PRO WRESTLING LEGENDS

Steve Austin
The Story of the Wrestler They Call "Stone Cold"

Bill Goldberg

Ric Flair
The Story of the Wrestler They Call "The Nature Boy"

Mick Foley
The Story of the Wrestler They Call "Mankind"

Bret Hart
The Story of the Wrestler They Call "The Hitman"

Billy Kidman

Lex Luger
The Story of the Wrestler They Call "The Total Package"

Vince McMahon Jr.

Shawn Michaels
The Story of the Wrestler They Call "The Heartbreak Kid"

Kevin Nash

Pro Wrestling: The Early Years

Pro Wrestling's Greatest Matches

Pro Wrestling's Greatest Tag Teams

Pro Wrestling's Greatest Wars

Pro Wrestling's Most Punishing Finishing Moves

Randy Savage
The Story of the Wrestler They Call "Macho Man"

The Story of the Wrestler They Call "Chyna"

The Story of the Wrestler They Call "Diamond" Dallas Page

The Story of the Wrestler They Call "Hollywood" Hulk Hogan

The Story of the Wrestler They Call "The Rock"

The Story of the Wrestler They Call "Sting"

The Story of the Wrestler They Call "The Undertaker"

Jesse Ventura
The Story of the Wrestler They Call "The Body"

The Women of Pro Wrestling

CHELSEA HOUSE PUBLISHERS

Pro Wrestling: The Early Years

Matt Hunter

Chelsea House Publishers
Philadelphia

Produced by Chestnut Productions and Choptank Syndicate, Inc.

Editor and Picture Researcher: Mary Hull
Design and Production: Lisa Hochstein

CHELSEA HOUSE PUBLISHERS

Editor in Chief: Sally Cheney
Associate Editor in Chief: Kim Shinners
Production Manager: Pamela Loos
Art Director: Sara Davis
Director of Photography: Judy L. Hasday

Cover Photos: Jeff Eisenberg Sports Photography
                and AP/Wide World Photos

The Chelsea House World Wide Web site
address is http://www.chelseahouse.com

First Printing

1 3 5 7 9 8 6 4 2

Library of Congress Cataloging-in-Publication Data

Hunter, Matt.
    Pro wrestling: the early years / Matt Hunter.
       p. cm. — (Pro wrestling legends)
    Includes bibliographical references (p.) and index.
    ISBN 0–7910–6455–7 (alk. paper) — ISBN 0–7910–6456–5 (pbk. : alk. paper)
       1. Wrestling—History—Juvenile literature. [1. Wrestling—History.] I. Title. II. Series.

    GV1195.3 .H87 2001
    796.812—dc21

                                                                00–069412

Contents

CHAPTER 1
THE ROOTS OF WRESTLING   7

CHAPTER 2
THE FIRST TELEVISION ERA   15

CHAPTER 3
STRENGTH OF THE 1960s   25

CHAPTER 4
SENSATION IN THE '70s   33

CHAPTER 5
THE RISE OF WCW   43

CHAPTER 6
THE PAY-PER-VIEW ERA   53

Chronology   61

Further Reading   62

Index   63

THE ROOTS OF WRESTLING

What are the roots of wrestling? In some respects, asking that question is the same as asking, "What are the roots of breathing?" or "What are the roots of eating?" It's an impossible question to answer, because as long as there have been living creatures on the planet, there has been wrestling.

All you need to do is look at a pair of newborn puppies playing in the dirt; that's a form of wrestling. Look at animals in the wild: young lions and bear cubs "wrestle" as a form of play. Older animals also battle for territory and use these "matches" to determine supremacy.

The earliest men living in caves no doubt "wrestled" each other for the best part of the cave or the tastiest morsels of food. The rules of sport weren't established yet, of course, and the physical skills were as raw as could be. Still, the notion of one man pitted against another, relying on their wits and physical ability, is as old as humankind.

In this sense, wrestling is the purest form of sport there is.

There is a reference to wrestling in Genesis, the first book of the Bible. In Genesis Chapter 32, Verses 25–26 read: "So Jacob was left alone, and a man wrestled with him until the break of dawn. When the man saw that he could not

---

Ed "Strangler" Lewis, left, puts Ed Don George in a headlock during their January 7, 1935, bout in New York City. Lewis began wrestling in 1903, when he was 13 years old and won his first world title in 1917 at the old Madison Square Garden.

An illustration of a 19th century London wrestling match depicts fans getting involved in the action while a boy works the crowd, selling apples to onlookers.

overpower him, he struck Jacob's hip at its socket, so that his hip was wrenched as he wrestled."

Wrestling was first developed as a formal sport in ancient China and Egypt. In ancient Greece, wrestling was part of every young man's education and every soldier's training. Greek sculpture, murals, and vases frequently bear images of two men wrestling, and in Greek literature wrestling is described as the sport of gods and kings as well as soldiers and common men.

The 18th ancient Olympic Games, held in 704 B.C., included wrestling. To win an ancient wrestling match, an athlete needed to throw his opponent to the ground three times, making him land on his hip, shoulder, or back. As in the modern version of the sport, biting was not allowed. Attacking one's opponent by breaking his fingers, however, was allowed.

Wrestling in England and the United States grew in popularity throughout the late-1700s and the 1800s. In 1764, Richard Carew of London published *The Survey of Cornwall,* in which he described English wrestling in detail. Various areas of England had their own styles. Wrestlers in Cornwall wore short jackets and gripped each other's arms and shoulders as in judo, while wrestlers in Lancashire wore tight jackets or underwear and stood apart with their knees bent and arms outstretched. According to Carew, kicking and pinching, as well as the pulling of hair and the twisting of arms and fingers, was not allowed.

There are many well-known stories of young Abraham Lincoln, who would go on to become the 16th president of the United States, engaging in wrestling matches. In 1831 Lincoln moved to New Salem, Illinois, at the age of 22. A group of young men known as "the Clary's Grove boys" lived nearby, and often boasted that they were the best wrestlers in Illinois.

At the time, Lincoln was working as a store clerk, and the owner of the store boasted that Abe, at 6' 4" and 185 pounds, was a better athlete than anyone he knew. Indeed, Lincoln was an excellent wrestler as well as a fine runner and boxer. The boasts got back to Jack Armstrong, the leader of the Clary's Grove boys, who challenged Lincoln to a wrestling match. Lincoln accepted.

The entire town came out for the match. Townspeople placed bets on the outcome of the match (the owner of the store in which Lincoln worked bet $10 that Abe would win), and the match was on. Lincoln got the better of Armstrong, and when his victory angered the other Clary's Grove boys, he offered to take them on one at a time. Impressed by Lincoln's courage, Armstrong stepped forward and shook his hand.

According to some versions of the match, the bout ended with Lincoln saying, "Jack, let's quit. I can't throw you. You can't throw me." In any case, Lincoln and Armstrong shook hands and became friends.

At about this time, Irish immigrants were bringing the "collar and elbow" style of wrestling to New England. The name comes from the stances the participants take as defenses against kicking, punching, and rushing. The style became widespread during the Civil War, and ultimately formed the basis of many American pro wrestling techniques. Meanwhile, in Paris, France, wrestling was banned in 1856 after officials discovered that many matches were fixed. The ban caused many French athletes to move to Belgium, Greece, and the United States.

America's Frank Sexton, top, puts former Italian world heavyweight boxing champion Primo Carnera in a footlock during a 1947 match.

Wrestling in the United States first began to enjoy widespread popularity in the late 1800s, following a surge of popularity in England and Scotland. In 1880, three years after defeating French champion Christol for the Greco-Roman championship, William Muldoon triumphed over Thiebaud Bauer and became the first famous U.S. wrestling champion. Typically, the money to be made in wrestling was done via side bets. The official purses were small: $7 would go to the winner, while $3 would go to the loser.

By the early 1900s, wrestling and boxing were both popular sports in the United States, with early wrestling champions of the century including George Hackenschmidt (1904), Frank Gotch (1908), Ed "Strangler" Lewis (1920), and Gus Sonnenberg (1929). Tag team wrestling was introduced in San Francisco in 1901 as a way of increasing the sport's entertainment value, but the idea didn't catch on elsewhere until the 1930s.

During the first few years of the 20th century, Hackenschmidt won championship tournaments in Italy, Germany, and England. On May 5, 1904, a match was held in New York between Hackenschmidt and American champion Tom Jenkins. Hackenschmidt won the bout in two straight falls. While there were various claims to world championship status by various athletes, just as there are today, Hackenschmidt was most widely viewed as the first legitimate world champion of the century. He defended his claim as champion for nearly four years, until he walked out of the ring and refused to return during an April 3, 1908, bout against Frank Gotch in Chicago.

The early part of the 20th century was a boom time for wrestling. In 1911, for example, Gotch and Hackenschmidt battled each other in Chicago's Comiskey Park. Tickets for the event, which saw Gotch take three straight falls, cost anywhere from $1 to $10—and drew a gate of $87,053, indicating a live attendance worthy of any major pay-per-view event today!

Other major stars of the first half of the 20th century included Lou Thesz (who won his first world title in 1937 and would go on to win five more world titles—the last in 1963), Jim Londos (who made his pro debut in 1917 and

During his 39-year ring career, Ed "Strangler" Lewis, shown in a 1924 photo, wrestled in 6,200 matches and won the world heavyweight wrestling championship five times. Lewis always preferred grappling to show business and once said of the wrestler Gorgeous George, "I wouldn't know whether to throw him or kiss him."

applied what is presumed to be wrestling's first sleeperhold, to the head of Ray Steele, in a 1931 match in Yankee Stadium in front of 21,000 fans), and Jim Browning (a world champion who was such a national celebrity, he appeared in national ads for Adam Pantera Hats alongside sports legends of the day like boxer Jack Dempsey and baseball star Carl Hubbell).

Stars in other sports crossed over to wrestling. Bronko Nagurski, a well-known football star, captured two world titles, in 1939 and 1941. Primo Carnera, a heavyweight boxing champion, took up wrestling in 1941 at the age of 34. Even baseball legend Babe Ruth entered wrestling, albeit as a referee, in 1945.

As popular as the sport was throughout the first half of the 20th century, wrestling was about to undergo an incredible explosion of interest due to something that was rapidly changing life all across America—television.

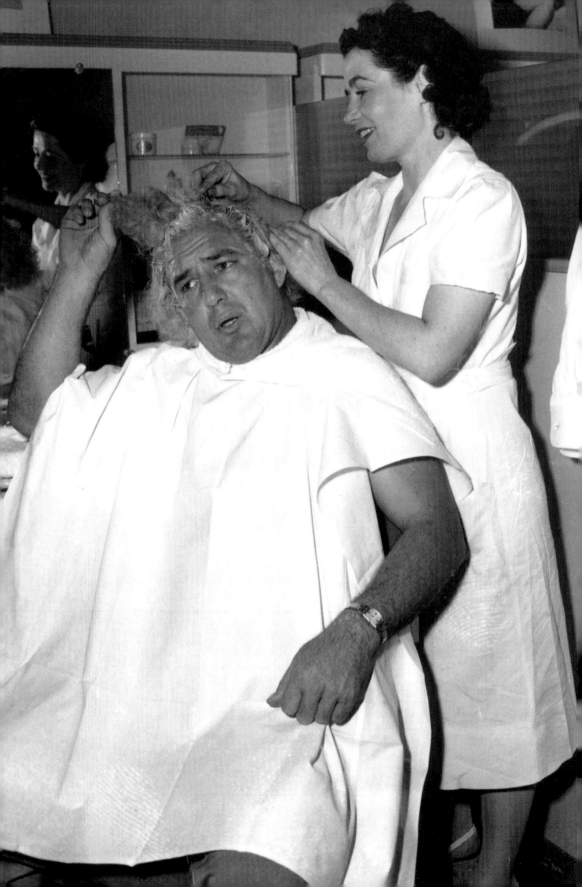

2 | THE FIRST TELEVISION ERA

The first regularly scheduled television broadcasts in North America actually happened in 1929, but it took a while for this new medium to become a familiar fixture in households across the United States. By 1936, there were only about 2,000 television sets in use worldwide.

Television sets were first made available to consumers in 1938, but it wasn't until after the end of World War II, as soldiers returned home and families began settling back into the routines of daily life, that television made its impact felt. By 1948, about a million homes in America were equipped with a TV set.

The late 1940s saw an explosion of interest in the new medium. *The Howdy Doody Show* began airing in 1947, the same year that the World Series was first shown on TV. Milton Berle's *Texaco Star Theater*, one of the most popular TV shows of all time, debuted in 1948.

And, of course, there was professional wrestling.

Dick Lane in Los Angeles, California, holds the distinction of broadcasting the first televised wrestling matches. The first "star" of televised wrestling, though, was not one of the athletes, but was one of the sport's first broadcasters: Dennis James. An employee of the DuMont Network, James

Gorgeous George gets his hair bleached at a Hollywood beauty salon in 1948. One of the first wrestlers to appear on television, George was known for his preening: he always wore his blond mane perfectly curled, and he made his valet spray perfume in the ring before every match.

broadcast television's very first commercial and went on to become nationally known as a game show host. He was also the host of the United Cerebral Palsy telethons for nearly 50 years.

James's style as a wrestling announcer was a far cry from the broadcasters of today. Where today's broadcasters often have a deep knowl-edge of the intricacies of the sport, James was a complete novice. Mere hours before his first broadcast as a wrestling announcer in 1946, James scrambled to the New York Public Library, checked out six books about wrestling, and skimmed them on the taxi ride to the arena, located in Jamaica, Queens, just across the river from New York City.

What James lacked in substance, though, he more than made up for in style. In addition to stopping off at the library on the way to the arena, James stopped at a butcher shop and bought a bag of chicken bones. He also brought a rubber dog toy to the arena. As a wrestler was caught in a bone-snapping hold, James would in turn snap one of the chicken bones into the microphone. When a wrestler took a punch, James accentuated the impact by slapping the dog toy into his palm in perfect time to the move in the ring. The result was to bring an element of humor to the proceedings, an element that resonated strongly with the viewers at home.

As Michael Ritchie writes in his book *Please Stand By: A Prehistory of Television*, the direc-tor of James's broadcast, Lou Sposa, "knew that this was a turning point in television his-tory. DuMont immediately became New York's number one sports station." Wrestling at the Jamaica Arena was a sensation. James added

Gorgeous George models his new haircut and one of his more than 100 robes in this photograph from 1954. George called himself "the human orchid" because his elaborate coiffure and clothing resembled the showy flower.

to his sound effects repertoire after that initial broadcast, using a harmonica when a wrestler was thrown out of the ring, and rubbing balloons together to simulate moans and groans of pain.

It was the first time wrestling and broadcast success went hand in hand, but it certainly wouldn't be the last. Meanwhile, television stations nationwide saw the success of televised wrestling in New York and scrambled to get wrestling programs of their own on the air.

If James's antics at the broadcast table were seen as outrageous by television viewers, they were nothing compared with the never-before-seen-or-imagined actions of the first mat

Antonio Rocca, facing camera, gets caught in a cradle crab hold by Lou Thesz during a March 24, 1953, match at Madison Square Garden. A former South American heavyweight wrestling champion, Rocca was a graduate of the University of Vincenza Treviso and spoke six languages.

superstar of the early television era: "Gorgeous" George.

Born in 1915, in Seward, Nebraska, George Wagner began wrestling when he was about 14 years old, but it wasn't until he was 24 that he developed the persona that would make him famous worldwide as the "Toast of the Coast," the "Sensation of the Nation," and "the Human Orchid."

Wrestling had always been known as a sport for the most rugged of men, usually the kind of men who were ragged around the edges, chomped cigars, and were known to have been in as many street fights as sanctioned athletic contests. So when Gorgeous George arrived on the scene, smaller than most wrestlers at 190 pounds and sporting bleached-blond hair, he caught everyone's attention. But it was more than hair that was different about him. He demanded that the ring—and his opponents—be sprayed with perfume before he would even think of climbing through the ropes.

At a time when no "real man" would be caught dead wearing anything even remotely frilly, Gorgeous George paid in the neighborhood of $1,000 each for the frilliest and fanciest robes he could find to wear as he strutted to the ring. Of course, George wouldn't put the robe on himself; that was beneath him. That simple task was left to one of the valets—Geoffrey or Thomas Ross, for example—who accompanied him to the ring.

George not only pioneered outrageousness in the sport, he was also the first to use entrance music, strutting to the ring to the sounds of "Pomp and Circumstance," the same music later used by "Macho Man" Randy Savage.

Gorgeous George was both infuriating and fascinating. Fans hated him, but they couldn't get enough of him. The television camera loved George as much as he loved it. It's been said that aside from Milton Berle, Gorgeous George was responsible for selling more television sets in the early days of TV than anyone else.

George's first televised entrance to the ring on a bed of rose petals, on November 11, 1947, was ranked number 45 in the top 100 "Greatest Moments in Television" by *Entertainment Weekly* magazine.

Above all, the outrageousness meant ticket sales. Promoters discovered that when Gorgeous George was on the card, attendance skyrocketed. In 1949, when New York's famed Madison Square Garden brought wrestling back to the arena after an absence of 12 years, Gorgeous George was the headline attraction.

Gorgeous George was a role model for future athletes and entertainers. Many years after George made his first televised strut to the ring, legendary boxer Muhammad Ali would credit his own outspoken persona to Gorgeous George's use of flamboyant theatrics. Singer James Brown, who borrowed George's habit of wearing a cape, also owes a stylistic debt of gratitude to "the Human Orchid."

While he didn't capture many championships (he didn't have to!), Gorgeous George did hold the American Wrestling Association (AWA) World title in 1950. That championship was merged with the National Wrestling Alliance (NWA) World title on July 27, 1950, when NWA World champion Lou Thesz defeated Gorgeous George in Chicago.

Gorgeous George's most famous match took place on November 7, 1962. George bet his treasured blond hair against the mask of the Destroyer. George lost the match—and was shaved bald!

Truly the first sports entertainment celebrity, Gorgeous George's life outside of the ring was as flamboyant as it was between the ropes. He seesawed several times between wealth and poverty, was married and divorced twice, and died of a heart attack in his Hollywood apartment the day after Christmas, 1963. He was 48 years old.

To say that Gorgeous George was the only real wrestling star of the 1950s; however, would do a tremendous disservice to the many talented athletes and champions of the decade. Lou Thesz, for example, held the NWA World title twice during the decade, including one title reign that lasted from July 1948 until March 1956. Verne Gagne, who would go on to form a new version of the AWA in 1960, held the NWA U.S. title for an astounding 31 straight months before being upended by Wilbur Snyder in April 1956. Danny Hodge, a superb amateur grappler who gained notoriety in the pro ranks as a seven-time NWA junior heavyweight champion, appeared on the cover of *Sports Illustrated* magazine in 1957.

There were many others, too. Indeed, two of the biggest box office draws of the decade,

Gorgeous George was one of the first showmen of pro wrestling, and he set an outrageous tone for the sport that continues to this day.

aside from Gorgeous George, were "Nature Boy" Buddy Rogers and Antonino Rocca.

Rogers is acknowledged as one of the first wrestlers to combine showmanship with quality wrestling. He incorporated high-impact maneuvers like the piledriver into his repertoire, and he was the first to effectively utilize what would become his signature finishing hold, the figure-four leglock. In 1961 and 1963, Rogers was the only man to hold both the NWA and World Wide Wrestling Federation (WWWF) World titles. In 1992, Ric Flair, another "Nature Boy," who modeled himself after Buddy Rogers, became the second wrestler to hold both titles. Flair's brash and cocky style won him millions of admirers and detractors.

Antonio Rocca, meanwhile, was the kind of athlete in whom few fans could find fault. "In the ring, I try to transmit the desire to smile," said the humble athlete who was born in Treviso, Italy.

Rocca is the only wrestler ever to receive the Carnegie Medal, which he won at the age of 16 after saving the life of a fellow swimming contestant during a race in Rome's Tiber River.

Rocca later moved to Argentina where he became a heavyweight wrestling champion and married one of Buenas Aires's most prominent socialites.

An excellent soccer player, Rocca found a way to use his kicking skills in the ring, popularizing the dropkick. When Vince McMahon Sr., father of current WWF owner Vince McMahon Jr., promoted his first wrestling event in New York's Madison Square Garden, Rocca headlined the card. A true sportsman, Rocca appreciated his success and gave back to the community that supported him. He spent much of his free time working with charities, especially those that aided sick children.

As the 1950s drew to a close, the sport of wrestling thrived, thanks to the antics of showmen like Dennis James and Gorgeous George, and the skills of athletes like Antonio Rocca and Buddy Rogers. Television gave wrestling a boost in popularity, and vice versa. Now it was time for wrestling to re-establish itself on a grass roots regional level.

3

STRENGTH IN THE 1960s

L
ooking back to the 1960s, some wrestling fans may feel that it was a time in the sport when things were dull, a time that nothing of significance happened.

Nothing could be further from the truth.

In the 1960s, the sport remained true to its roots, and in fact strengthened those roots considerably. Thriving regional promotions were created. Several enduring wrestling stars were in the prime of their careers. While the world at large seemed, in many people's eyes, to be going insane with the war in Vietnam, political assassinations, and the rise of youth counterculture, wrestling was a sport that remained true to itself and provided reliable stability to its fans.

THE AMERICAN WRESTLING ASSOCIATION

In August 1960, the AWA was formed. It's first world champion was Verne Gagne, a successful amateur wrestler who competed at the University of Minnesota and at the 1948 Olympic Games. A successful light heavyweight wrestler in the pro ranks (he held the NWA junior heavyweight title in 1958), Gagne was, in mid-1960, enormously popular in the Midwest, and was viewed as the uncrowned champion in the sport. When the Minnesota-based AWA was formed, Gagne

Announcer Jimmy Lennon raises the arm of Pedro Morales in victory after Morales defeated the Destroyer for the world heavyweight wrestling championship on March 13, 1965, in Los Angeles.

was the logical choice to become its first champion and standard-bearer.

It was the first time in the United States since the NWA was formed in 1948 that the sport boasted two sanctioned and widely recognized world champions: Verne Gagne and Buddy Rogers.

The AWA quickly grew to become one of the most powerful regional promotions in the sport. At the height of its strength, the AWA promoted wrestling cards not only throughout Minnesota, but also in Illinois, Nebraska, Nevada, and Utah—even as far west as California and as far north as Winnipeg, Manitoba, in Canada.

During the 1960s, Gagne held the AWA World title eight times, defeating such legendary and rugged grapplers as Gene Kiniski, the Crusher, Mad Dog Vachon, and Fritz Von Erich. Gagne's eighth title reign, which began on August 31, 1969, when he defeated "Dr. X" Dick Beyers in Minneapolis, Minnesota, lasted an incredible seven years and two months before he was defeated by Nick Bockwinkel in St. Paul, Minnesota, on November 8, 1975.

An honorable champion and a favorite of AWA fans, Gagne exerted an enormous influence on the sport behind the scenes. He helped train such legendary wrestlers as "Nature Boy" Ric Flair, Rick Steamboat, "Mr. Perfect" Curt Hennig, the Iron Sheik, Bob Backlund, Sergeant Slaughter, Ken Patera, and Baron Von Raschke.

THE WORLD WIDE WRESTLING FEDERATION

Less than three years after the AWA was formed, the sport underwent a major change— all because of a single match between two men in Toronto, Ontario, Canada.

On January 24, 1963, Lou Thesz defeated NWA World champion Buddy Rogers in one fall during a match in Toronto. He was awarded the NWA World title, but a group of promoters based in the Northeast—including Vince McMahon Sr.—refused to recognize the title change as valid. They broke away from the NWA and formed the WWWF—the World Wide Wrestling Federation. (In 1979, the second "W" would be dropped, and the promotion would become known as the World Wrestling Federation, or WWF.)

Rogers, the Nature Boy, was the first WWWF World champion, having defeated

"Living Legend" Bruno Sammartino, center, worked as a wrestling commentator after retiring from the ring.

Antonio Rocca in the final match of a tournament in Rio de Janeiro, Brazil, in April 1963. It was Bruno Sammartino, however, who ruled the WWWF and the Northeast pro wrestling scene in the 1960s and beyond.

On May 17, 1963, Sammartino and Rogers stepped into the ring in New York's Madison Square Garden. The atmosphere among the fans was not unlike the seventh game of a World Series or the final quarter of a close Super Bowl game. The Nature Boy was the most hated man in the sport at the time, while Sammartino, a charismatic wrestler and weightlifter from Abruzzi, Italy (and later Pittsburgh, Pennsylvania), could seemingly do no wrong. He did no wrong that night. After a series of dropkicks, a bearhug (Sammartino's favorite hold), and an "Italian backbreaker," a new WWWF champion was crowned.

The match lasted just 48 seconds. The title reign lasted nearly eight years.

"Judging from the enormous reaction [in the arena] that night, I knew my future was bright," the champion who would quickly become known as "The Living Legend" told *Inside Wrestling* magazine. "I was young, and that victory gave me confidence. Wrestling hadn't been doing too well in New York at the time, but selling out [Madison Square] Garden became the norm after that match."

In the sports world of the 1960s, Bruno was as much a celebrity as Mickey Mantle or Willie Mays—and he made as much money as his baseball counterparts. During his prime years with the WWWF, which continued into the late-1970s, Sammartino headlined Madison Square Garden 211 times—187 of those cards were standing-room-only sellouts. Chants of "Bru-no! Bru-no!" were heard not just in the Garden, but in packed arenas throughout the Northeast, from Boston to Baltimore and Philadelphia to Pittsburgh.

The legend of "the Living Legend" grew with each remarkable match and feud. As Sammartino met and defeated a veritable Who's Who of pro wrestlers in the 1960s—Haystacks Calhoun (Sammartino actually bodyslammed the 601-pound behemoth!), Gorilla Monsoon, Waldo Von Erich, Killer Kowalski, George "the Animal" Steele, Fred Blassie—the influence and power of the WWWF grew along with Sammartino's reputation.

Sammartino was knowledgeable in the technical aspects of the sport, but he was often pitted against the most heinous rulebreakers the WWWF could find. As a result, his wrestling style was based mainly on his strength. His personal style, though, was based on passion, and in every televised interview, that passionate love not just for the sport, but also for his fans, came through loud and clear.

In the Northeast in the 1960s, pro wrestling and Bruno Sammartino were one and the same.

OTHER REGIONS—OTHER STARS

While the formation and rise of the AWA and the WWWF were certainly the two biggest stories in the sport in the 1960s, the NWA was certainly not to be ignored. Only five men wore the NWA World heavyweight championship belt throughout the decade, a stunning testament to the ability of each champion.

Pat O'Connor began the 1960s as NWA titleist, having won the belt from Dick Hutton in January 1959. O'Connor was defeated by Buddy Rogers in June 1961, then Lou Thesz captured his sixth NWA World title from Rogers in January 1963. Gene Kiniski upended Thesz in January 1966, and wore the belt until February 1969, when he lost it to Dory Funk Jr., whose reign lasted more than four years.

It was Dory Funk Jr., in fact, who did the most to make his title a world title in this decade. On December 2, 1969, Dory defended his belt against Japanese legend Antonio Inoki. The two men battled to a 60-minute draw in the first NWA World title match held in Japan in 12 years.

Elsewhere in the United States, Portland Wrestling in Oregon, led by promoter Don Owen, continued to go strong, just as it had

Dory Funk Jr., shown getting a bearhug from Superstar Graham, was NWA World champion from 1969 to 1973 and defended his title against Japanese wrestling star Antonio Inoki.

since 1948, featuring such 1960's notables as Mad Dog Vachon, Stan Stasiak, Moondog Mayne, Pat Patterson, Nikolai Volkoff, and Pepper Martin.

In California, meanwhile, the World Wrestling Association (WWA) was turning Los Angeles into a great city for pro wrestling. WWA champions during this time included Edouard Carpentier, Fred Blassie, the Destroyer, Pedro Morales, and Bobo Brazil.

In Texas, Fritz Von Erich defended the World Class Texas American title against such stars as Johnny Valentine, the Spoiler, and Brute Bernard, laying the groundwork for the astounding success that the Von Erichs—the "First Family of Wrestling"—would enjoy in the 1980s.

Other top stars of the era included Dick the Bruiser, whose toughness was displayed before 10,000 fans in Detroit in 1963 when he suffered a five-stitch wound over his right eye on the way to the ring, where he beat football player Alex Karras; Jackie Fargo, who helped popularize Tennessee-area wrestling throughout the decade; and Ray Stevens, a high-impact grappler who favored the piledriver and a jump off the top rope called the "bombs away."

The decade saw the pro debuts of many stars who would go on to define the sport in the 1970s. Masked legend Mil Mascaras debuted in 1964, and NWA World champion Jack Brisco debuted in 1965. Also debuting in 1964 was Andre the Giant, one of the sport's biggest stars—literally and figuratively—who would become one of the mat game's defining personalities in the decade to follow.

4

SENSATION
IN THE '70s

He was born Andre Roussimoff on May 19, 1946, and made his pro wrestling debut in 1964 in France as "The Butcher." He was 6' 3" and 200 pounds at the age of 12, and as a grown man stood 7' 5" and weighed 525 pounds at his heaviest. In 1971, he made his Canadian debut at Verdun, in Quebec. But it wasn't until he began wrestling in the WWWF in 1973, that the career and legend of Andre the Giant began to grow to giant proportions.

What made Andre a giant was a condition known as acromegaly. The excessive secretion of growth hormones caused progressive enlargement of his head, face, hands, feet, and chest. It slowed Andre down in later years, but it never sapped his spirit. Rather than a man to be pitied, Andre was a celebrity to be admired.

"I have had good fortune," Andre said. "I am grateful for my life. If I were to die tomorrow, I know I have eaten more good food, drunk more beer and fine wine, had more friends and seen more of the world than most men ever will."

Early in his career, Andre weighed closer to 400 pounds and was able to stun opponents and fans alike with an occasional dropkick. He traveled the country, never staying long in any one regional promotion, but winning legions of

The late Andre Roussimoff, better known as Andre the Giant, made his American wrestling debut in the 1970s and remains one of the most popular and best loved wrestlers of all time.

fans in all areas of the United States. Wrestling fans knew that if their local hero ever got into trouble with the bad guys terrorizing their region, Andre the Giant could be called in to straighten things out and save the day!

"The whole world is his circuit," Vince McMahon Sr., who owned the WWWF and served as Andre's personal booking agent in the 1970s, told *Sports Illustrated* magazine in 1981. "By making his visits few and far between, he never becomes commonplace. Now, wherever he goes the gates are larger than they would be without him. I book him for three visits a year to Japan, two to Australia, two to Europe, and the rest of the time I book him into the major arenas in the U.S. The wrestlers and promoters all want him on their cards because when the Giant comes, everyone makes more money."

As indicated in McMahon's quote, Andre's fame spread far beyond U.S. wrestling rings. He was an enormous star in Canada and Japan, and it's been said that during his heyday, Andre was the second most recognized human on the planet, behind Muhammad Ali.

Andre was just one major spectacle in a decade during which the sport was learning how to promote itself on a grander scale than ever before. As the second most recognized human on the planet, it was only fitting that he participate on the undercard of a wrestling event that involved the first most recognized human on the planet.

On June 26, 1976, boxer Muhammad Ali and wrestler Antonio Inoki squared off in a boxer vs. wrestler contest in Tokyo, Japan. The match was a worldwide sensation, with ringside seats selling for $1,000 each. In the United

States, 32,000 fans were on hand to see the match via closed-circuit television, as well as another boxer-wrestler bout, between Chuck Wepner and Andre the Giant, and a bout between Stan Hansen and Bruno Sammartino. (Hansen had broken Sammartino's neck two months earlier.)

That wrestling could be highlighted on such a massive scale was something that was never before imagined, much less accomplished. The fact that the match was horrible—a 15-round draw that could best be described as "dreadful"—didn't matter. It may have taken custodians a full day to clear all the garbage that was hurled at the ring in Budokan Hall, but the notion of professional wrestling as worldwide spectacle is something that has lasted to this day and will no doubt continue for many, many years to come.

Muhammed Ali and Japanese wrestler Antonio Inoki face off during the fourth round of their boxer vs. wrestler match held in Tokyo on June 26, 1976. The match was a draw.

Andre the Giant, right, holds boxer Chuck Wepner in a bearhug prior to tossing him out of the ring at Shea Stadium for a third round victory on June 26, 1976.

Spectacle aside, wrestling as a sport continued to be healthy and to grow in stature and popularity during the 1970s. There were still many regional promotions around the country. The Portland, Oregon promotion continued to attract top talent like Jimmy Snuka and Jesse Ventura. Texas wrestling saw the rise of stars such as Blackjack Mulligan and Blackjack

Lanza, as well as Bruiser Brody and Big John Studd, who also frequented the St. Louis, Missouri, region. Memphis, Tennessee, was featuring stars like "Boogie Woogie Man" Jimmy Valiant and Jerry "The King" Lawler. By and large, however, the U.S. wrestling scene was settling into a "big three" framework that included the WWWF, the AWA, and the NWA.

In the WWWF, Ivan Koloff became the most hated man in the sport by dethroning Sammartino from nearly eight years as champion. Koloff only held the belt for a few weeks, followed by Pedro Morales, who reigned for nearly three years. The impact of Morales on the WWWF was considerable. A popular star, he had often competed in the shadow of the more-popular Sammartino. But when he won the title, he proved to the fans—and to himself—that he could stand alone and headline cards without Sammartino.

The two men remained friends, even though they wrestled each other on a famous card in New York's Shea Stadium. On September 30, 1972, approximately 35,000 fans were on hand to witness Pedro defend the world title against the Living Legend. It was one of Sammartino's greatest matches ever, and certainly the greatest of Pedro's career. The two battled to a 75-minute curfew draw, but Pedro was clearly the winner: Not only had he retained his title, he had proven himself equal to the man who personified wrestling in the Northeast.

When Stan Stasiak dethroned Morales on December 1, 1973, however, Bruno seized the opportunity to wrestle him nine days later and won. The second coming of Sammartino added another 3 1/2 years to his overall tenure as

WWWF World champion and cemented his legend as an all-time great.

The AWA World title was a rare example of championship stability: Verne Gagne won his eighth AWA World title in August 1968, and remained champion until he was upended by Nick Bockwinkel in November 1975. The decade ended with Bockwinkel still champion (Gagne regained the belt in July 1980).

In the NWA, the world title was bouncing back and forth among a group of rugged, hard-nosed competitors: Dory Funk Jr., the rough-and-tumble with superb scientific skills who was regarded as the last of the truly noble NWA champions; Harley Race, who held four of his eight NWA World titles in the 1970s and defended the title outside the boundaries of the United States more than any other champion before or since, making the NWA World title truly a world title; Terry Funk, the brother of Dory Funk Jr. whose wild brawling style brought him a 14-month title reign beginning in December 1975, in which he absorbed as much punishment as he dished out; and Jack Brisco, who wore the belt twice, holding the title continuously between July 1973 and December 1975, with the exception of a one-week title loss to Japanese superstar Shohei "Giant" Baba.

During the 1970s, the NWA was an alliance among a group of promotions in the United States and overseas. Regional promotions in Florida, Oregon, and Missouri, for example, were members of the NWA. That meant that the NWA World champion would occasionally travel to the regional territory to defend his championship against the top regional champion.

One of the strongest members of the NWA at this time was Jim Crockett Promotions, which had been formed in 1935. The promotion held cards in the Mid-Atlantic region, North Carolina, South Carolina, Virginia, and Georgia. When Jim Crockett Sr. retired in 1973, his son, Jim Crockett Jr., took over the promotion, changing the name from Eastern States Championship Wrestling to Mid-Atlantic Championship Wrestling.

Harley Race won the NWA World title eight times. After retiring from professional wrestling, Race founded the Race Academy and became CEO of World League Wrestling. In the late 1990s he spoke out against the profanity and extreme violence that seemed to have taken over the sport.

Mid-Atlantic Championship Wrestling was a powerhouse, and during the 1970s it boasted a veritable galaxy of wrestling stars. Mid-Atlantic heavyweight champions during the decade included: Jack Brisco, Jerry Brisco, Ole Anderson, Wahoo McDaniel, Ric Flair, Greg Valentine, Ken Patera, and Tony Atlas. Other stars in the Mid-Atlantic region were Roddy Piper, Dusty Rhodes, Rick Steamboat, Jimmy Snuka, Blackjack Mulligan, and Paul Orndorff.

A smaller promotion, Georgia Championship Wrestling, was also a member of the NWA. In 1972, the program *Georgia Championship Wrestling* began broadcasts on Atlanta station WTCG. The TV show was hosted by Gordon Solie and Les Thatcher and featured a wide range of regional and nationally known stars battling over the Georgia heavyweight and tag team titles.

During the latter half of the 1970s, Georgia heavyweight champions included Dusty Rhodes, the Spoiler, Dick Slater, Mr. Wrestling II, Paul Jones, Stan Hansen, Angelo Mosca, Wahoo McDaniel, and Masked Superstar. On the tag team side, championship duos included Jimmy and Johnny Valiant, Gene and Ole Anderson, Tommy Rich and Tony Atlas, and Jack and Jerry Brisco. There was nothing going on in Georgia Championship Wrestling to distinguish it from regional promotions elsewhere in the country, except that it was in the right place at the right time.

In the 1970s, a young Atlanta-based media mogul named Ted Turner was pioneering something called the "superstation"—an independent broadcast station whose signal is picked up and redistributed by satellite to local cable television systems. Station WTCG was renamed WTBS in 1976, and, by 1979, SuperStation WTBS was featuring *Georgia Championship Wrestling* at 6:05 on Saturday nights. As it had in the 1950s, the medium of television once again transformed the mat sport.

5 THE RISE OF WCW

A once-in-a-lifetime series of wrestling and broadcast events combined to create the phenomenon known as World Championship Wrestling (WCW). Most significant was the fact that by the late-1970s, cable television was beginning to make inroads into homes from coast-to-coast. Local cable television outlets were eager to provide programming variety as an enticement for viewers to subscribe to cable, and one of the most popular channel choices became SuperStation WTBS in Atlanta, Georgia.

By 1979, Saturday nights on WTBS brought a national audience a wrestling program called *Georgia Championship Wrestling.* For the first time ever, a regional promotion was being seen on a national scale, and wrestling fans couldn't get enough. It didn't matter to fans who would never visit Georgia that the broadcast spent a good portion of its time talking about the next wrestling card in Atlanta's Omni arena. This was something new, different, and fresh! For many fans nationwide this was a chance to finally see for themselves the wrestlers they had only read about in the magazines or heard about from friends who had cable television.

Georgia Championship Wrestling was in the right place—Atlanta—at the right time—the expansion of cable television.

"Nature Boy" Ric Flair, who modeled himself after Buddy Rogers, the original Nature Boy, benefited from the growth of the NWA and WCW and became one of the biggest stars of both federations.

But the promotion became a phenomenon because it rose to the occasion. The opportunity for national exposure was there, and Georgia Championship Wrestling responded with the best-produced wrestling broadcast of the day.

The Saturday night TBS broadcast originated at a well-lit television studio in Atlanta, not a dark arena. The atmosphere was aided by a few hundred enthusiastic fans allowed into the studio each week, and their energy was remarkably infectious for the viewer at home, who felt like they had a ringside seat to the proceedings.

Presiding over it all was Gordon Solie, the broadcaster who became known as "the Dean of Wrestling Broadcasters" and "the Walter Cronkite of Professional Wrestling." Solie's importance to the success of wrestling on TBS in the early 1980s cannot be overlooked. Where Dennis James in the mid-1940s entertained audiences by cracking chicken bones, Solie enthralled audiences by offering them a style that approached every event happening inside the ring (and often outside of it as well) and every comment made by a wrestler at the interview podium (no matter how blatantly absurd or ridiculous) with a seriousness and respect that wrestling had seldom known. Solie was authoritative and knowledgeable. He rarely tried to be cute or clever, and he never tried to overshadow the wrestlers themselves. He was the perfect anchorman for taking *Georgia Championship Wrestling* national, because he possessed that most cherished of broadcast assets: credibility.

"During my years in college and my years in minor league baseball, I used to watch

WTBS at 6:05 p.m. every Saturday," veteran WCW broadcaster Tony Schiavone recalled upon Gordon's death in 2000. "I would imagine working alongside Gordon. I would practice commentating with him, as I would talk to my TV during those two hours on TBS."

Fans felt the same kinship with the program and Solie. It didn't take long for Saturday nights on TBS to become must-see television for any serious wrestling fan. By 1982, the TBS broadcasts were being used as a platform for testing the waters of national expansion. Georgia Championship Wrestling cards were promoted in Ohio, Pennsylvania, and West Virginia. Also that year, the two-hour broadcast was renamed *World Championship Wrestling* to reflect its popularity and national scope.

That larger scope attracted a remarkable level of talent to the TBS studios during this time. "Nature Boy" Ric Flair, "American Dream" Dusty Rhodes, Tommy "Wildfire" Rich, Junkyard Dog, Ted DiBiase, "Rowdy" Roddy Piper, the Fabulous Freebirds, "Mr. Wonderful" Paul Orndorff, and Jake "the Snake" Roberts all gained national prominence as the result of appearing on TBS. Because the broadcast was national and not regional, the wrestlers tended to give everything they had, and then some, when they appeared on TBS. Saturday night wrestling from Atlanta consistently had the best wrestlers, the most energetic matches, and the most entertaining interviews seen anywhere on television.

Announcer Gordon Solie was instrumental to the success of Georgia Championship Wrestling's first television broadcasts in the 1980s.

To understand the kind of star-making influence the TBS broadcast had in the early 1980s, consider the example of the Road Warriors.

In the summer of 1983, Hawk and Animal, accompanied by their manager, "Precious" Paul Ellering, burst onto the TBS scene. Wrestling had never seen anything like them. Muscular and powerful, the Road Warriors wore unusual face paint. Animal sported a Mohawk haircut, while Hawk sported a reverse-Mohawk. They didn't walk up to the ring and drink in the boos of the fans, as every bad guy wrestler or team had done before them. Instead, they sprinted to their match, stormed the ring

With help from TBS, WCW, and their manager Paul Ellering, center, the Road Warriors rose to the top of the tag team wrestling scene in the 1980s.

without waiting for the bell, slid under the bottom rope at high speed, and pummeled their opponents senseless.

They dominated, and they made an incredible impression on fans everywhere. On Monday mornings, at school and in the office, the wrestling chatter was often about what the Warriors had done the previous Saturday night. Though they had only wrestled professionally for about half the year, the Warriors were named Tag Team of the Year by the readers of *Pro Wrestling Illustrated* magazine.

Without the national stage of TBS and the *World Championship Wrestling* program powering their supercharged entry into the sport, the Warriors might never have had the chance to reshape tag team wrestling in the 1980s into their own violent image.

World Championship Wrestling became a springboard not only for creating national stars and testing the waters of promotion boundaries, but also for a concept known as the "supercard." Jim Crockett Promotions and Georgia Championship Wrestling worked in close cooperation with each other, so in the fall of 1983, *World Championship Wrestling* broadcasts began discussing something that promised to be a major event for the sport: the first of the NWA's Starrcade cards. The event was to be held on November 24 in Greensboro, North Carolina, but would also be made available at closed-circuit locations throughout the Mid-Atlantic region.

The main event of the card saw "Nature Boy" Ric Flair capture his second NWA World heavyweight title by defeating Harley Race. It was the first time that the NWA championship had ever changed hands in a steel cage match. In two other memorable bouts, Rick Steamboat and Jay Youngblood dethroned Jack and Jerry Brisco to become NWA World tag team champions, and "Rowdy" Roddy Piper defeated Greg "the Hammer" Valentine in a bloody and brutal dog collar chain match. Starrcade was a major success, drawing 15,447 NWA faithful to the Greensboro Coliseum, and an additional 30,000 fans to closed-circuit locations.

Meanwhile, a major feud was brewing—and not between two wrestlers or tag teams. This one would be between two warring promotions, and would continue into the beginning of the next century.

Since the heyday of Bruno Sammartino, the idea of the WWF vs. the NWA had always been something of a friendly feud. Fans would argue over whose roster was better and compare the relative merits of each world champion. Occasionally, those champions would actually compete against each other. On July 4, 1982, for example, WWF World champion Bob Backlund and NWA World champion Ric Flair met at the Omni in Atlanta. The bout ended in a double-disqualification after about 20 minutes of furious action. Two years after the Backlund-Flair bout, another major WWF vs. NWA battle took place in Atlanta. This time, the arena was not the Omni, but TBS.

While Georgia Championship Wrestling had been testing the waters of national promotion by expanding beyond its traditional territory, its cards in Ohio and Pennsylvania didn't threaten other major regional promotions. The WWF, by contrast, was making moves in 1983 that not only outraged the regional promoters

(who traditionally observed unwritten agree-
ments to never invade each other's territories),
but were a hint of an even more aggressive
expansion to come. In September, the WWF
promoted a card in California, in what had
traditionally been AWA territory. Later in the
year, the WWF scored a major coup by signing
the AWA's most popular and promising star:
Hulk Hogan.

In April 1984, the WWF started broadcasting
a two-hour show on the USA cable network.
Tuesday Night Titans was widely seen as the
WWF's answer to *World Championship Wrestling*
on TBS. The NWA responded by promoting the
first card of NWA wrestling in the New York area
in 20 years with its "Night of Champions" on
May 29 at the Byrne Meadowlands Arena in
New Jersey.

Then came black Saturday.

In 1984, Vince McMahon Jr., owner of
the WWF, purchased Georgia Championship
Wrestling. Fans tuning in to the July 14, 1984,
broadcast of *World Championship Wrestling*
expecting to see Gordon Solie and their favorite
NWA wrestlers battling in the TBS studio were
shocked as they were greeted by McMahon,
who introduced taped WWF matches. More than
1,000 phone calls of complaint flooded the TBS
switchboard that weekend. But McMahon would
not budge. In an interview with the *Atlanta
Constitution*, he said "We'll show those com-
plainers the difference between a major league
and a minor league promotion, given time."

TBS tried to appease viewers with a new
Saturday morning program, *Championship
Wrestling from Georgia*. The show was a ratings
success. Amidst all this activity, the Universal

Wrestling Federation (UWF) began running a program on TBS as well, starting in March 1985, but the program only lasted a few months.

Meanwhile, the war between the two federations was in full swing. The WWF was countering Starrcade with WrestleMania. Mid-Atlantic Wrestling had joined with several other promotions to create *Pro Wrestling USA*, which was syndicated to local television stations, and also aired on the sports cable channel ESPN. The WWF was making bigger strides, however, with wrestling programs on cable's MTV and network television's NBC. Those strides proved costly though, and in April 1985, Vince McMahon Jr., in need of cash to fuel the aggressive national expansion of the WWF, decided to sell the TBS time slot to Jim Crockett for $1 million. Crockett went on to sell Jim Crockett Promotions to TBS owner Ted Turner in November 1988. Crockett Promotions was renamed World Championship Wrestling (WCW) and a McMahon vs. Turner feud, one of the sport's longest-lasting rivalries in or out of the ring, began.

The seeds of the WWF-NWA/WCW war had been planted. They had sprouted not just an enormous amount of animosity between the two organizations, but also an explosion of national interest in the mat sport, the likes of which had never been seen before.

It was a war the WWF was clearly winning. When *Sports Illustrated* ran a cover story on pro wrestling in April 1985, it was WWF star Hulk Hogan, not WCW/NWA star Ric Flair, who appeared on the cover. In May 1985, when pro wrestling returned to network television for the

6 THE PAY-PER-VIEW ERA

Like Jim Crockett, Vince McMahon was the son of a successful regional wrestling promoter. Like Crockett, McMahon purchased the promotion from his father (in June 1982) and saw bigger things for the sport.

Unlike Crockett, McMahon was willing to break all the rules to achieve his goals. McMahon invaded other promoters' territories to hold wrestling cards of his own. He paid local television stations to air his programs, often setting up the deal in such a way that the regional promoter's television show would be relegated to a less-desirable time slot. He raided talent from other promotions, luring top stars away with promises of big paychecks and national fame. One of those stars was Hulk Hogan.

In 1982, Hogan was nowhere on the wrestling scene. He had competed in the WWF briefly as a rulebreaker in 1980 and 1981, but at this point in his life he was almost ready to quit the sport when he called Verne Gagne, the former AWA World champion who owned the Minneapolis-based promotion.

"When he called me, I didn't know who he was," Gagne recalled in an Internet interview for *Slam! Wrestling*. "He called from Tampa, Florida. I said, 'Look, who are you?' He said, 'I'm Hulk Hogan.' Greg [Verne's son] happened to be in

Vince McMahon stands in front of a poster of Hulk Hogan during a 1985 press conference. Hogan was the kind of colorful, exciting wrestler McMahon wanted to cultivate in his federation.

The Iron Sheik represented all the evil forces that opposed the United States, and Hulk Hogan became an American hero when he defeated him on January 23, 1984. Hulkamania soon swept the nation.

my office. I said to him, 'Greg, have you ever heard of a guy by the name of Hulk Hogan?' And he said, 'Yeah, I saw him in New York one time.' I said, 'How was he?' He said, 'Ah, so-so.' He said, 'He's a big guy.' So I said 'Okay.' Then I'm back talking to Hogan. He said, 'I'd like to give it one more try. I've quit wrestling 'cause I can't make it. But I'd like to give it one more shot. I've been sitting here for the last three weeks or a month, and could I come into the AWA?' So we brought him up, and the rest is history."

Hogan quickly became a top star in the AWA, feuding with world champion Nick Bockwinkel, but he never had the chance to hold the title. In late 1983, the WWF saw the potential in Hogan and signed him to a contract.

On January 23, 1984, Hogan battled WWF World champion the Iron Sheik in New York's Madison Square Garden. The match was not without significant controversy: Bob Backlund was scheduled to wrestle the Sheik, as it was the Iranian rulebreaker who had ended Backlund's 5 1/2-year WWF World title just a month earlier. Hogan hadn't even wrestled a match in the WWF when he was declared the number-one contender to the belt and given the match against the Sheik.

Those who were in the Garden that night described the atmosphere in the air as electric. Those who have seen the match have described it as a massacre. In just 5 minutes and 40 seconds, Hogan dismantled the Iron Sheik, legdropped him for the three-count pinfall victory, and captured the WWF World title.

Hulkamania was born.

This was more than another wrestler winning another title. Hogan possessed incredible charisma. The fans supported him, and that support seemed to cut across all age groups. The sport was eagerly looking for its next big superstar, and Hogan was it—and then some. The "Hulkster" was not a great technical wrestler by any means, but he was a riveting personality made for television—and just the character the WWF needed to spearhead its national expansion.

With Hogan as champion, the WWF grew in popularity at a rate never before seen in the sport. On February 18, 1985, "The War to Settle the Score"—a match between Hogan and Roddy Piper—was broadcast live on MTV. On April 29 of that year, Hogan appeared on the cover of *Sports Illustrated*. On May 11, Hogan battled "Cowboy" Bob Orton as the WWF presented *Saturday Night's Main Event* on NBC, marking the return of wrestling to network television after an absence of 30 years.

It seemed like every week, Hogan and the WWF were setting new records for the sport and making new inroads into popular culture.

Nothing else the WWF did in the mid-1980s captured the public's imagination like Wrestle-Mania. March 31, 1985, saw the WWF promote its first WrestleMania card. The main event was Hogan and Mr. T battling Roddy Piper and Paul Orndorff at Madison Square Garden in New York City. The event was packed with celebrities, including Muhammad Ali, Liberace, and

Joan Rivers. In the weeks leading up to the match, Hogan and Mr. T were seen everywhere, from MTV to *Saturday Night Live.*

The first WrestleMania card was not available on pay-per-view television. Wrestling's first pay-per-view card happened about seven months later, on November 7, 1985, as the WWF presented its "Wrestling Classic" from the Rosemont Horizon in Chicago.

The card is largely forgotten by wrestling fans today. Aside from a title bout that saw Hogan defending his WWF World title against Roddy Piper (the Hulkster won by disqualification when "Cowboy" Bob Orton interfered), the entire card consisted of a tournament that was ultimately won by Junkyard Dog, who defeated "Macho Man" Randy Savage in the final round.

Pay-per-view television is tailor-made for pro wrestling, which has long been a creature of television. A promotion can spend hours upon hours of traditional television time building up anticipation for the big event, then charge anywhere from $14.95 to $29.95 per home to see the pay-per-view card. Instead of promoting the next big card at the local arena for only local fans to see, the television broadcasts promote the next big pay-per-view event for everyone across the country to see.

In 1986, the WWF presented wrestling's second pay-per-view event: WrestleMania II, which was held in not one, but three arenas: Nassau Coliseum in Long Island, New York, the Rosemont Horizon in Chicago, and the Sports Arena in Los Angeles, California.

When 1987 rolled around, the WWF doubled its pay-per-view output that year, offering two cards. WrestleMania III was held on March 29 at the Silverdome in Pontiac, Michigan. The main event saw Hogan retain his WWF World title by pinning Andre the Giant in front of a crowd of 93,173 fans, a North American live attendance record for the sport that stands to this day.

The NWA responded to the WWF's moves in the pay-per-view arena by airing Starrcade '87 via pay-per-view, but the WWF was fiercely defending its territory: it held the Survivor Series on November 26, 1987—the same day as Starrcade.

The sport's use of pay-per-view television grew swiftly: Seven pay-per-view cards were presented in 1988, including one by the AWA. By 1995, the number of pay-per-view cards available to the wrestling fan had increased to 20. In 1997 the number had risen to 28, and in 1999 the sport as a whole presented 33 pay-per-view events—an average of one every 11 days!

The bottom-line attraction of pay-per-view television for wrestling's promoters can be seen by looking at one very successful card: Starrcade '97.

The main event of Starrcade '97 was a match between former WWF megastar Hulk Hogan and WCW star Sting. The suggested retail price for viewing Starrcade was $29.95, and it was estimated that 625,000 homes purchased the event, for a total sales of nearly $19 million. WCW called it the biggest event in their history. In fact, it was the third most popular pay-per-view event of any kind that year, beaten only by two boxing matches.

By the end of the 1990s, the "must-see" television evening changed from Saturday night to Monday night, and the focus of the events

Andre the Giant battles Hulk Hogan at WrestleMania IV. Andre/Hogan bouts were huge draws for the WWF in the late 1980s.

seen on television changed from the local live card to the next pay-per-view event. The sport as a whole had changed again, driven by the technology known as pay-per-view television.

Yet in looking at the early days of the sport, it is clear that wrestling and television have always had a very close relationship. In the 1940s and 1950s, the rise of television in American homes created the sport's first major rise in popularity and the sport's first major celebrity: Gorgeous George. In the late-1970s and early 1980s, the rise of cable television in American homes created the first truly national wrestling promotion: Georgia Championship Wrestling. In the 1990s, the rise of pay-per-view television in American homes created a new way of promoting the mat sport and funneled millions of dollars into the coffers of the two major promotions: WWF and WCW.

As the sport moves into the 21st century, one can't help but wonder how emerging new technologies will change pro wrestling. It's happening already: The Internet is allowing wrestling fans to exchange information at an astounding rate of speed. Where once a wrestling fan needed to wait two months to read about a major wrestling event in a national wrestling magazine, now fans can enter a chat room and discuss a pay-per-view card as it is happening.

What's next? Will the computer converge with television and create new opportunities for the sport to continue to expand and grow? Will outcomes of wrestling matches be dictated by fans watching at home and interacting in some way with the program and the wrestlers themselves? Will pay-per-view television give way to Internet broadcasts of major wrestling events?

These are all fascinating questions. Given the rapid pace of change over the last decade, both in the sport of wrestling and in the growth of technology, one thing is certain: There's never been a better time in history to be a wrestling fan.

Chronology

1904   George Hackenschmidt defeats Tom Jenkins in New York to become the first widely recognized legitimate world champion of the century on May 5

1931   Wrestling's first sleeperhold is applied to Ray Steele by Jim Londos during a match in Yankee Stadium

1935   Jim Crockett Promotions is formed

1946   Dennis James broadcasts his first wrestling match, for the DuMont network. His cracking of chicken bones during matches helps televised wrestling become enormously popular

1948   The NWA is formed

1960   The AWA is formed in August

1962   Gorgeous George loses a match to the Destroyer on November 7 and has his treasured blond hair cut off

1963   The WWWF is formed

1964   Andre the Giant makes his pro debut in France

1972   Georgia Championship Wrestling begins broadcasts on television station WTCG in Atlanta

1982   Georgia Championship Wrestling is renamed World Championship Wrestling

1984   On July 14 the WWF takes over the WCW time slot on TBS. Fans call it black Saturday

1985   WrestleMania I is held at Madison Square Garden in New York City on March 31; On May 11 pro wrestling returns to network television after an absence of 30 years as the WWF's *Saturday Night's Main Event* airs on NBC; the WWF's Wrestling Classic becomes the first-ever pay-per-view card on November 7

1988   Ted Turner purchases Jim Crockett Promotions in November and renames the organization World Championship Wrestling

1990   The AWA folds in December

1999   A total of 33 pay-per-view wrestling cards are held, 24 more than were held a decade earlier, in 1989

Further Reading

Editors of London Publishing. *Inside Wrestling Presents The 100 Greatest Wrestlers of the Century.* Ft. Washington, PA: London Publishing, 2000.

Editors of London Publishing. *Pro Wrestling Illustrated Presents the 2000 Wrestling Almanac and Book of Facts.* Fort Washington, PA: London Publishing, 2000.

Hunter, Matt. *Superstars of Men's Pro Wrestling.* Philadelphia: Chelsea House, 1998.

Hunter, Matt. *Wrestling Madness: A Ringside Look at Wrestling Superstars.* New York: Smithmark, 1999.

"Professional Wrestling: Year By Year" *Pro Wrestling Illustrated Presents the 1999 Wrestling Almanac and Book of Facts.* Ft. Washington, PA: London Publishing, 1999, pp. 110–151.

Ritchie, Michael. *Please Stand By: A Prehistory of Television.* Woodstock, New York: Overlook Press, 1994.

Index

Ali, Muhammad, 34, 55
Andre the Giant, 31, 33–35
Backlund, Bob, 48, 54
Beyers, Dick, 26
Blackjack Lanza, 36
Blackjack Mulligan, 36, 40
Blassie, Fred, 29, 31
Bockwinkel, Nick, 38, 54
Brisco, Jack, 31, 38, 40
Browning, Jim, 13
Calhoun, Haystacks, 29
Carnera, Primo, 13
Carpentier, Edouard, 31
Crockett, Jim, Jr., 39, 53
Crusher, the, 26
Ellering, Paul, 46
Flair, Ric, 22, 26, 40, 47,
  48, 50
Funk, Dory, Jr., 30, 38
Funk, Terry, 38
Gagne, Verne, 21, 25, 26,
  38, 53
Gorgeous George, 18–23, 58.
  See also George Wagner
Gorilla Monsoon, 29
Gotch, Frank, 11, 12
Hackenschmidt, George,
  11, 12

Hansen, Stan, 35, 40
Hodge, Danny, 21
Hogan, Hulk, 49–51, 53–57
Inoki, Antonio, 30, 34
Iron Sheik, the, 54, 55
James, Dennis, 15–17, 23,
  44
Jenkins, Tom, 11
Killer Kowalski, 29
Kiniski, Gene, 26, 30
Koloff, Ivan, 37
Lane, Dick, 15
Lawler, Jerry, 37
Lewis, Ed, 11
Lincoln, Abraham, 9, 10
Londos, Jim, 12
Mad Dog Vachon, 26, 31
Mascaras, Mil, 31
McMahon, Vince, Jr., 22,
  49, 50, 53
McMahon, Vince, Sr., 22,
  27, 34
Morales, Pedro, 31, 37
Nagurksi, Bronko, 13
O'Connor, Pat, 29
Orndorff, Paul, 55

Orton, Bob, 55, 56
Owen, Don, 30
Patterson, Pat, 31
Piper, Roddy, 55, 56
Race, Harley, 38, 47
Road Warriors, the, 46, 47
Rocca, Antonio, 22–23, 28
Rogers, Buddy, 22–23, 26,
  27, 30
Sammartino, Bruno, 28,
  29, 35, 37, 48
Snuka, Jimmy, 36, 40
Solie, Gordon, 40, 44, 45,
  49
Sonnenberg, Gus, 11
Stasiak, Stan, 31, 37
Sting, 57
Thesz, Lou, 12, 20, 27, 30
Turner, Ted, 40, 50
Valentine, Johnny, 31
Valiant, Jimmy, 37, 40
Ventura, Jesse, 36
Von Erich, Fritz, 26, 31
Wagner, George, 18.
  See also Gorgeous George
Wepner, Chuck, 35

Photo Credits

Associated Press/WWP: pp. 6, 12, 14, 18, 21, 24, 35, 36, 45; Corbis/Bettmann: pp. 17, 52; Jeff Eisenberg Sports Photography: pp. 2, 32, 39, 42, 54, 58, 60; David Fitzgerald: pp. 30, 46; Howard Kernats Photography: p. 27; Library of Congress: pp. 8, 10.

MATT HUNTER has spent nearly two decades writing about professional wrestling. In addition to this book on pro wrestling, the author's previously published volumes on the mat sport include *Jesse Ventura: The Story of the Wrestler They Call "The Body,"* *The Story of the Wrestler They Call "Hollywood" Hulk Hogan, Superstars of Pro Wrestling*, and *Wrestling Madness*. He has interviewed countless wrestlers on national television, photographed innumerable bouts from ringside, and written more magazine articles about the mat sport than he cares to calculate.